Beautiful World

**Copyright © 2017
by Sandeep Ravidutt Sharma**

All rights reserved. No part of this book may be reproduced or transmitted in any form or by any means without written permission from the author.

If you have further questions, contact on

**Phone: +919969256731
Email: sandeepraviduttsharma@gmail.com**

Cover photo courtesy: Shashikala Sharma

Dedication

This book is dedicated to **Lord Vishnu** who is the Supreme Self, the preserver and the protector of the universe. Vishnu is the "preserver" in the Hindu trinity that includes Brahma and Shiva.

To please **Lord Vishnu** praying for the well being, victory and success of my readers in their endeavour, i hereby recite the following mantra...

"Om Namo Bhagavate Vasudevaya"

"Om Shri Hari Vishnu Vasudevaya Namah"

© Beautiful World
BY SANDEEP RAVIDUTT SHARMA

Table of Contents

Foreword I

Beautiful World..1

© Beautiful World
BY SANDEEP RAVIDUTT SHARMA

Foreword

This book provides you with a list of 100 positive, inspiring and motivating thoughts churned out by my mind with the grace of **Lord Vishnu**.

I'm sure if you keep reading, referring and sharing these thoughts and quotes, you will draw inspiration and it would motivate you to take your next step forward towards achieving success and happiness in your life.

"Beautiful world exists right within your beautiful mind."

I sincerely hope, you will find this book amazing, interesting, rejuvenating, unique and a constant source of Inspiration.

Thank You and Happy Reading.

Beautiful World

© **Beautiful World**
BY SANDEEP RAVIDUTT SHARMA

If you want love, hug and cheers, remember it's a two way process.

© Beautiful World
BY SANDEEP RAVIDUTT SHARMA

Glamour attracts you but reality adores you.

© **Beautiful World**
BY SANDEEP RAVIDUTT SHARMA

Truth needs a good listener who understands well.

© Beautiful World
BY SANDEEP RAVIDUTT SHARMA

Everyday remember to wear your million dollar smile and stay positive.

© **Beautiful World**
BY SANDEEP RAVIDUTT SHARMA

Be happy with whatever you have. God has chosen it specially for you.

© **Beautiful World**
BY SANDEEP RAVIDUTT SHARMA

Zero expectations can make you happy forever.

© **Beautiful World**
BY SANDEEP RAVIDUTT SHARMA

Delayed success is better than accidental one.

© **Beautiful World**
BY SANDEEP RAVIDUTT SHARMA

First and the last step are the most crucial ones to achieve success.

© **Beautiful World**
BY SANDEEP RAVIDUTT SHARMA

Fight not to dominate others but win their hearts.

© **Beautiful World**
BY SANDEEP RAVIDUTT SHARMA

Don't measure progress only in terms of money.

Just by tying the hands of the clock, you can't stop the forward march of time.

What you see is what you get in life. Don't just see isolation and loneliness but a colourful backdrop of happiness all around.

© **Beautiful World**
BY SANDEEP RAVIDUTT SHARMA

To reach your destination you may choose to drive a car or walk. In no way it affects your destination.

© Beautiful World
BY SANDEEP RAVIDUTT SHARMA

Live or leave an opportunity. Choice is all yours.

© Beautiful World
BY SANDEEP RAVIDUTT SHARMA

Drop of happiness multiplies and becomes an Ocean when shared.

© Beautiful World
BY SANDEEP RAVIDUTT SHARMA

Don't make noise if you are not ready to hear the same from others.

© Beautiful World
BY SANDEEP RAVIDUTT SHARMA

Life is complete only when you have experienced both happiness and grief, prosperity and poverty, love and hatred, innocence and maturity, and many more.

© Beautiful World
BY SANDEEP RAVIDUTT SHARMA

The secret of happiness resides right in your beautiful mind. No one can make you happy unless you want to be.

Smile likes your beautiful face.

© Beautiful World
BY SANDEEP RAVIDUTT SHARMA

You are million times better than your mirror image or photograph. Just believe in your own self.

© Beautiful World
BY SANDEEP RAVIDUTT SHARMA

You don't have to stop walking when it rains. Just find a way and you can walk again in the rains. Same way, walk over life challenges by finding a way out.

© Beautiful World
BY SANDEEP RAVIDUTT SHARMA

Time fails everyone. Make the most out of your time.

Positive thoughts forces depression and anxiety to run.

© Beautiful World
BY SANDEEP RAVIDUTT SHARMA

Never lie unless it is meant to make a person laugh or heal.

© Beautiful World
BY SANDEEP RAVIDUTT SHARMA

Wait is universal. Everything or everyone is waiting for someone or something in this world. Don't wait endlessly, instead reach out and meet.

Pack your bags well before you decide to board a Ship.

© Beautiful World
BY SANDEEP RAVIDUTT SHARMA

Good times are always there for those who are looking for it.

© Beautiful World
BY SANDEEP RAVIDUTT SHARMA

Castle of Sand are washed out during high tide. Build your dream house with strength of Stone and glue of love.

© **Beautiful World**
BY SANDEEP RAVIDUTT SHARMA

Don't make haste unless life is at stake.

© Beautiful World
BY SANDEEP RAVIDUTT SHARMA

Don't rent your happiness, do enough to own them.

© **Beautiful World**
BY SANDEEP RAVIDUTT SHARMA

Carry your baggage without any expectations of help from others.

Keep faith in your own self before expecting the world to do so.

© Beautiful World
BY SANDEEP RAVIDUTT SHARMA

Your shadow many a times walks ahead of you, so why expect others to follow you always.

© Beautiful World
BY SANDEEP RAVIDUTT SHARMA

Challenges of life always appear to be big. Face them with grit and determination, sooner they turn into OPPORTUNITIES.

© **Beautiful World**
BY SANDEEP RAVIDUTT SHARMA

Unlock your positive thoughts and experience the AMAZING world.

© Beautiful World
BY SANDEEP RAVIDUTT SHARMA

Real world doesn't offer you the privilege to walk on an illuminated path always. Learn how to tread carefully even on a dark pathway.

© Beautiful World
BY SANDEEP RAVIDUTT SHARMA

No one can sit with misunderstanding. TALK IT out soon.

© Beautiful World
BY SANDEEP RAVIDUTT SHARMA

Expect if you like but RESPECT the outcome.

© **Beautiful World**
BY SANDEEP RAVIDUTT SHARMA

Prove yourself right without trying to find faults in others.

© Beautiful World
BY SANDEEP RAVIDUTT SHARMA

Good thoughts invite GOOD times.

© **Beautiful World**
BY SANDEEP RAVIDUTT SHARMA

Good times serve pleasantness in life.

© Beautiful World
BY SANDEEP RAVIDUTT SHARMA

You lose once after accepting failure but quitting is loss forever.

© Beautiful World
BY SANDEEP RAVIDUTT SHARMA

Life makes you LAUGH and cry.

Positivity emerges as a bright Moon in your character and illuminates not just your life but others as well.

Crisis are no more when your mind is in control.

© **Beautiful World**
BY SANDEEP RAVIDUTT SHARMA

The path of happiness passes through the jungle of challenges. Face them and you are through.

© **Beautiful World**
BY SANDEEP RAVIDUTT SHARMA

Expectations pulls you down when you lose focus on your efforts.

© **Beautiful World**
BY SANDEEP RAVIDUTT SHARMA

There is no retake in life. Give your best always.

Every failure makes you more experienced and mature enough to ensure that it's not repeated again.

© Beautiful World
BY SANDEEP RAVIDUTT SHARMA

Those who are addicted to manipulation don't even leave their near and dear ones. Never manipulate others just for the sake of achieving SUCCESS.

© **Beautiful World**
BY SANDEEP RAVIDUTT SHARMA

Pen your pain to share and seek solution from the experienced ones.

© Beautiful World
BY SANDEEP RAVIDUTT SHARMA

Practice SILENCE to tame your anger.

© **Beautiful World**
BY SANDEEP RAVIDUTT SHARMA

Dreams make you FLY even without wings.

© **Beautiful World**
BY SANDEEP RAVIDUTT SHARMA

Don't meet someone as King or a Beggar, be HUMAN.

© Beautiful World
BY SANDEEP RAVIDUTT SHARMA

To hate someone is easy but to love someone is much easier. All you have to do is exchange SMILE as token of your love.

You alone have to keep turning the smiling WHEEL of happiness.

© **Beautiful World**
BY SANDEEP RAVIDUTT SHARMA

The flow of life never stops. Just pay attention and you can be part of the flow.

© Beautiful World
BY SANDEEP RAVIDUTT SHARMA

Moon thwarts dark forces every night and inspires the Stars to do their bit.

© **Beautiful World**
BY SANDEEP RAVIDUTT SHARMA

Truth is fire. It can burn as well as purify the courier and the recipient.

© **Beautiful World**
BY SANDEEP RAVIDUTT SHARMA

Pain disappears in front of Smile.

© **Beautiful World**
BY SANDEEP RAVIDUTT SHARMA

Storm of thoughts can turn upside down your life boat if you don't apply your MIND and sail in the right direction.

© **Beautiful World**
BY SANDEEP RAVIDUTT SHARMA

EARN your freedom and not just beg for it.

© Beautiful World
BY SANDEEP RAVIDUTT SHARMA

Nothing is more precious than your NEXT breath.

© Beautiful World
BY SANDEEP RAVIDUTT SHARMA

Expectation is the root cause of bitterness and unhappiness around you. It's better to ACCEPT than expect to ensure constant flow of happiness.

© **Beautiful World**
BY SANDEEP RAVIDUTT SHARMA

Real teacher is interested in the well being of his disciple rather than waiting for monetary benefit.

© **Beautiful World**
BY SANDEEP RAVIDUTT SHARMA

*Fight or fright.
Choice is all yours.*

© **Beautiful World**
BY SANDEEP RAVIDUTT SHARMA

Friendship is a two way COMMITMENT.

© **Beautiful World**
BY SANDEEP RAVIDUTT SHARMA

Illuminate the world with your golden THOUGHTS and deeds.

Give your best to get the BEST.

© **Beautiful World**
BY SANDEEP RAVIDUTT SHARMA

Grab Opportunity in time and don't expect it to knock again.

© **Beautiful World**
BY SANDEEP RAVIDUTT SHARMA

Walking alone is our destiny.

© Beautiful World
BY SANDEEP RAVIDUTT SHARMA

Music opens the door of JOY and happiness.

Accept failure and move on in life.

© **Beautiful World**
BY SANDEEP RAVIDUTT SHARMA

Experience the wind but anticipate the storm to take REFUGE in time.

Great characters don't feel shy even if they have to BEG for helping others.

© Beautiful World
BY SANDEEP RAVIDUTT SHARMA

Live now and enjoy each MOMENT.

© **Beautiful World**
BY SANDEEP RAVIDUTT SHARMA

Everyone wants peace, happiness and freedom but very few remember to GIVE it back.

© Beautiful World
BY SANDEEP RAVIDUTT SHARMA

Beauty is forever for the person with good CHARACTER.

Don't try to find LOGIC in everything and everywhere. Many things in this world are beyond our reasoning.

© Beautiful World
BY SANDEEP RAVIDUTT SHARMA

It's our determination and WILL power that makes us work even in adverse situations.

© Beautiful World
BY SANDEEP RAVIDUTT SHARMA

It's quite natural to find faults in others. Instead why not try to look for POSITIVE traits in others.

© Beautiful World
BY SANDEEP RAVIDUTT SHARMA

Expect understanding from people who don't wear goggle of assumption and are not judgemental.

© **Beautiful World**
BY SANDEEP RAVIDUTT SHARMA

Hope never dies. It even knocks from behind a locked door.

© **Beautiful World**
BY SANDEEP RAVIDUTT SHARMA

Sun is the Ocean of positivity.

© **Beautiful World**
BY SANDEEP RAVIDUTT SHARMA

Walk away from those who no more listens to their heart and are always in speaking mode.

© **Beautiful World**
BY SANDEEP RAVIDUTT SHARMA

Learn to differentiate between what is real and unreal.

Hoping against hope which is drowning can keep you afloat.

© **Beautiful World**
BY SANDEEP RAVIDUTT SHARMA

Admit the guilt in time and you can rise again.

© Beautiful World
BY SANDEEP RAVIDUTT SHARMA

When a boat can float in the sea, we can also stay positive amidst sea of opportunities and threats.

© **Beautiful World**
BY SANDEEP RAVIDUTT SHARMA

Innocent souls can never even dream about cheating others.

© Beautiful World
BY SANDEEP RAVIDUTT SHARMA

When you love / like someone, even losing against them at times doesn't upset you. Follow the same rule with others and even major defeat in life can never pull you down.

© **Beautiful World**
BY SANDEEP RAVIDUTT SHARMA

Hopes for a bright and green future are alive.

Emotions cannot be held captive for long. Let it flow.

© **Beautiful World**
BY SANDEEP RAVIDUTT SHARMA

Truth needs courage and patience.

© Beautiful World
BY SANDEEP RAVIDUTT SHARMA

Make amends in your attitude if you find critics to be right about you.

© Beautiful World
BY SANDEEP RAVIDUTT SHARMA

Positive thinkers always look for solutions not just for them but for the world.

© Beautiful World
BY SANDEEP RAVIDUTT SHARMA

No one can stop the flow of positive light into your life if you have decided to embrace the same.

© Beautiful World
BY SANDEEP RAVIDUTT SHARMA

Hunger for money is good till the time you are going to spend it wisely and take care of the needy.

© **Beautiful World**
BY SANDEEP RAVIDUTT SHARMA

While you dream you don't have a choice. Face reality and decide what to remember or discard from your memory about your dream.

© **Beautiful World**
BY SANDEEP RAVIDUTT SHARMA

Laugh your way out of pain and sorrow.

www.ingramcontent.com/pod-product-compliance
Lightning Source LLC
Chambersburg PA
CBHW031438210526
45464CB00005B/2256